Zorba Books

Praise For
Be Safe in Cyberspace

This is the era of Science and Technology. Children are becoming tech savvy at a very young age and I strongly feel that their parents haven't kept up. In their enthusiasm to connect with people online, they freely access social networking sites. They go unescorted into cyber space, while we, adults, do not know how to protect them if they tread the wrong path. They are eager to be in-tune with the times and feel they are being 'modern'. Little do they realize that it can get them into trouble.

Children are unable to discern between the benefits and pitfalls of ever changing technology. Therefore instead of scaring them we need to empower them by creating awareness regarding the safe steps that should be followed while treading in cyber space.

In school a number of workshops are being held to make the children aware of the wrongs that are being committed on the Internet, wittingly or unwittingly and how to avoid and protect against such wrongs.

I would like to compliment Ms. Pooja Malhotra for this book that she has authored for the children. Very appropriate. This book beautifully covers different ways of using the Internet safely and wisely. The division of the book into different chapters each dealing with an important aspect of cyber safety makes the reading very specific in dealing with all individual concerns of the students. Cybercrimes under the Indian penal code have also been mentioned. The language is simple but interesting too. The analogies given in the book relate to the students very well.

This is a must read book for all children and I recommend that they read this book so they can enter into cyber space and be safe.

Suman Nath
Principal
Tagore International School
E Block, East of Kailash
New Delhi – 110 065
#9810533806

This is an excellent book on a topic which concerns most of us, as parents and educators - the uninhibited interest of our children in the Internet & its applications, with little awareness about the dangers it may pose, at times. The author has used jargon which can be easily understood by little children while the active usage of pictorial presentations adds to its essence.

Dr. Ruby Ahuja, Consultant Child Psychologist,
Mind Peace Psychiatry and DeAddiction Clinic,
Arya Neuropsychiatry Hospital,
Chandigarh.

In *Be Safe in Cyberspace,* Pooja Malhotra has dealt with a serious subject, and yet made it very interesting. In a slim volume, she has dealt with everything from cyber bullying and cheating to sexting, leaving out virtually nothing. The book is exhaustive but not exhausting; in fact it is un-put-down able, and you are likely to finish it in one sitting, although you are sure to go back to it repeatedly. The book is addressed to children, but is not only for children. Cybercrimes to which adults are susceptible, such as identity thefts and fake e-mails invoking either greed or compassion, find as much mention in the book as those of which the victims are more likely to be children. When dealing with the 'worldwide wolf' lurking in the worldwide web, we are all little Red Riding Hoods and need an empowering book like *Be Safe in Cyberspace* that combines judiciously the messages of caution and courage. The charming cartoons by Saswati Biswas bring to the book a touch of humour, which is an added bonus.

– **Dr. Ramesh Bijlani**, Former Professor, AIIMS, New Delhi;
Author of, among others,
Back to Health through Yoga (Rupa, 2008), *Eating Wisely and Well* (Rupa, 2012), and children's books *Our Body* (NBT, 1986), *The Return of Ram* (Scholastic, 2006) and *Kavya Makes Up Her Mind* (NBT, 2014)

BE SAFE IN CYBERSPACE

POOJA MALHOTRA

ZORBA BOOKS

Published in India by Zorba Books, 2015

Website: www.zorbabooks.com
Email: info@zorbabooks.com

ISBN 978-81-930152-7-8

Zorba Books Pvt. Ltd.(opc)
Gurgaon, INDIA

Cover design by Design Art Studio
Illustrator - Saswati Biswas

Printed in India

Dedicated to my children,

Vidur & Vrinda

Acknowledgement

The idea of writing this book came from my son's first faltering steps in cyberspace, wherein he unknowingly came across objectionable content. I started with helping him to be safe online and soon went on to interact with thousands of children across the city. The major guidelines in this book have been gained through my interactions with all of them. I thank them for their receptivity, openness, energy and zeal.

I feel indebted to my husband, Vishal Malhotra, who is my best friend, philosopher and guide! Without his constant motivation and loving support, this book would never have seen the light of day. I admire his fortitude in putting up with my procrastination.

I express my profound gratitude to Mrs. Anupa Lal, my teacher and mentor. I may not be her best student, but she is definitely my best teacher. I thank her for helping me and guiding me from start to finish. She has inspired me more than she will ever know!

I am grateful to Saswati Biswas for bringing the text to life with her innovative illustrations. I acknowledge her for her remarkable artwork, immense enthusiasm and promptness.

To my friends, parents and in-laws, who helped me in more than one ways, I offer my sincere gratitude.

Introduction

The advent of the Internet has transformed many aspects of our lives, including the way we communicate and the way we seek answers or collect information. As a student, I remember spending hours in the library trying to find relevant information for my school projects. Now with smart phones, laptops and electronic tablets, a large amount of information is available simply at the press of a button, and chatting, with a friend who lives on the other side of the globe, is just a few clicks away!

Though the Internet is a tremendously powerful tool offering a new way to connect with the world, it also harbours new risks – identity theft, privacy violations, cyber bullying, harassment by online predators, exposure to inappropriate material and much more.

An online predator is like the big, bad, hungry wolf in the Red Riding Hood story. He exhorted all the information from little Red Riding Hood, pretended to be her Granny, and when the unsuspecting Red Riding Hood walked into her Granny's cottage, he pounced on her.

This does not imply that we should stop accessing the fascinating world opening up before us; it simply means that the little Red Riding Hood should be aware of the dangers that lurk in the jungle called the 'world wide web' (www.). By simply being aware of the kind of dangers that exist, you can avoid getting into trouble and are able to safeguard yourself against such wolves and other predators hiding in the WWW.

The streets are buzzing with activity and fast cars zip past us as we try to cross the road. So do we stop moving out because we're scared of accidents? Of course not! We all know that eventually we all learn how to cross the street safely. The Internet is no different; we just need to be cautious and follow some simple safety rules. As you read further, you'll realize that just like following traffic safety rules can help avoid road accidents, following simple Internet safety rules can ensure online safety. So, read on and be safe in cyberspace!

Contents

1

SMART STEPS TOWARDS ONLINE SAFETY

Treating others the way you like to be treated is the foundation of all everyday activities including online activities. Sending hurtful or threatening messages to another person in cyberspace is easier since the computer screen provides a virtual wall to hide behind, but should be avoided.

Give Respect, Get Respect

Be careful with the words you use online, just the way you are when talking to a person face to face. Give respect, get respect!

On the contrary, if someone else's words make you uncomfortable (when online) ask them to stop. Be firm yet polite!

Pause before you post

Whatever happens in cyberspace remains in cyberspace...forever...

Unlike something that you write on the blackboard which you can rub or change, an online comment/ picture/video/email/blog once posted can never be removed. A few seconds after posting a comment, you might want to go back and delete it, but someone somewhere on the World Wide Web would have already read/copied/ downloaded/ forwarded your post. It's like putting up a notice on the school notice board and going back after some time to remove it, by then it would have been read by many people.

Before posting ask yourself:

- Who will be able to see my post?
- Will anyone feel hurt or embarrassed by it?
- Am I proud of what I'm posting?

- Will I be comfortable if my parents or teachers view my post?
- How would I feel if someone posted the same comment about me?

Always remember – There is no delete button on the Internet.

Pause before you post

Don't reveal personal information to Strangers

Before revealing personal information such as your address, phone number, school information, details about your parents' work place and sharing photographs, ask yourself the question - why are you being asked to give personal details? You would never give out such information to a stranger on the street. Follow the same practice when you are online.

Red Riding Hood would never have got into trouble had she not told the wolf that she was visiting her Granny, who lived at the other end of the forest. This simple example can help you to relate to the dangers of disclosing personal information to a stranger, while remembering that the age old advice “DON'T TALK TO STRANGERS" remains a golden rule even in the virtual world.

Don't reveal personal information

Block Messages from Strangers

Never open emails from unknown senders. Use settings on your email account to mark such email as 'spam' and simply delete these mails without opening them.

Similarly, use settings on Instant messaging programs to block messages from people you don't know.

Block messages from strangers

Visit 'Safe' websites – Look for the lock

To differentiate a safe site from a fake site, 'look for the lock'. Any website allowing safe transfer of information will display a 'secure green lock' icon somewhere on the browser. This icon is not just an image; you can click on it to view the security information of the site. Make sure that you check the functionality of the icon before you proceed.

Further, avoid visiting websites that are intended for adult viewing only. Such sites have content which could be offensive, violent, pornographic or even related to illegal activities, involving drugs or terrorism. Not only creating such sites, but also viewing them can land you in trouble.

Be cautious while downloading Apps

Downloading Apps may give App developers access to personal information that is not related to the purpose of the App. App developers may share the information they collect with marketing companies and other researchers. They can upload your contact lists and access your location and email, though in almost all cases you must give them permission to do so. They may also store personal and other sensitive information, and sell it or share it, without your knowledge.

Ensure that you check their privacy policy and your privacy settings to see what information the App developer can access. And consider this: You download an app to find out which cartoon character or movie actor you resemble, but is that momentary fun worth the danger of sharing your personal information with strangers? Why put yourself at risk?

Hyperlinks may lead you into trouble

It might be tempting to click on a potential 'great deal' or a 'not to be missed offer' or a humorous video. While most hyperlinks are quite safe, some lead you to trouble.

Sometimes people 'hijack' or take over a hyperlink and deliberately direct users to unsuitable material. If you follow a hyperlink while searching for information and it leads you to something offensive that makes you uncomfortable, close your browser immediately and report the matter to a trusted adult as soon as possible.

Hyperlinks can lead you into trouble

Install an Antivirus

Protect your computer against viruses by installing a good antivirus. Viruses not only harm the computer but can also lead to personal data theft. Your computer contains all the details of your identity and possibly, of your family and friends as well. It's very important to protect your system and keep it safe.

Install a good antivirus

2

SMART STEPS TOWARDS A STRONG PASSWORD

Creating a password can be a lot of fun! Passwords are secrets and secrets are not supposed to be easy to guess. Your password could be a unique combination of letters of the alphabet and numbers that don't make sense. For instance, you could drop the vowels from a long word (like juxtaposition) and replace them with numbers, then add a few symbols to create a strong password – (j5xt1p4s3t34n@#$ %)

A strong password can also be created using 6-8 characters – one character in small case, one in capitals, one number and one special character.

Create a strong password

Another idea is to choose a meaningful phrase with 6-8 words like 'I went to Disneyland 2 years ago!', pick the first letter of each word and insert a few symbols to get - IwtD2ya!@@

(Please don't use these examples as your passwords. Create your own ...and have fun!)

Don't Share your Password

Never reveal your password or personal identification number for any site to anyone, not even your best friend. The only exception should be your parents.

Sharing your password with your best friend creates a possibility that it may fall into the wrong hands in the future. If someone has your password, they can access your account and send nasty emails/messages on your behalf and turn your friend against you.

Don't share your password

Secure your Password

If you need to access the Internet in a public place, it is a must for you to secure your password after each use. Make sure that you sign out of your email/Facebook account at the end of your session.

Ensure that your password is not stored on your phone, since mobile phones are much more likely to be lost or stolen.

Secure your password

Use a different password for different websites

It is common for someone to steal your password and change your settings or lock your social media profile.

You might be tempted to use the same password for all your online accounts since it's easy to remember. The problem is - if someone figures out your password for one website, they will be able to access all your accounts using that one password.

So it is advisable to have different passwords for each email account/ social networking site/internet service that you access. This strategy will enable you to save the other accounts, even if one of your accounts has been hacked.

It might be a bit of a challenge to remember so many different passwords. An easy solution to this is to make a hand written list of all your passwords and hide it somewhere at home. Now you only need to remember where you've hidden your list!

Use different passwords for different sites

Don't "Save" your password

Certain websites offer an option of saving your username and password. If you 'Allow' the site to 'Remember your password' you can save a few seconds when you log in next time, but this can be dangerous. You should never use this option on a computer that is used by other people (such as the one in your school/college/Internet café) since anyone who gets access to the computer you have used can log on to your account automatically.

Don't save your password

3

SMART STEPS TOWARDS SAFE SOCIAL NETWORKING

You might be tempted to have a large number of friends (or as many as possible) on Facebook or other social networking sites but to stay safe online, you need to be selective while accepting friend requests.

Safe social networking

Don't accept friend requests from strangers. If you're too tempted to add them, put their name into a search engine and see what comes up. Make sure that you connect only with people you can trust.

The golden rule is – trust your instincts and don't befriend people whom you don't know offline!

Know your Privacy Settings

Most social networking sites offer very little protection if you use their default privacy settings. The moment you sign up, you need to go through and understand the privacy settings of the network (be it Facebook, Myspace, Pinterest, Google+, Twitter or any other social network). It is best to ensure that only 'friends' or specific people can access your personal information and view your profile & photographs.

Know your privacy settings

All online posts are essentially 'public'

There is no way to guarantee that what you post online will remain posted there. The Internet is like an 'information super highway' and whatever you post can travel anywhere – friends share 'private' messages, social networking sites change their privacy settings, Facebook accounts get hacked and email ids get stolen.

Before posting a picture, writing on a wall or sending a message, pause... and ask yourself if what you're sharing could be shared in public. If not, don't post it!

All online posts are public

Don't post personal details on social networking sites

Never post your home phone number mobile number or home address on any social networking platform. Everyone will be able to view your details and this can put you at a grave risk. Always think about the repercussions that your post might have before you click on 'Post'/'Send'.

Don't post personal details on social networking sites

Always enter your correct age

Don't say you're over 13 if you're not! You should know that a child under the age of 13 years (U13) is protected by the Children's Online Privacy Protection Act (COPPA). Essentially, COPPA protects a child's personal information from being collected and shared.

This legal protection can ensure your online safety, it will cover for you -if and only if- you mention your correct age. Just like your parents protect your younger siblings and take care that they don't get into trouble or get hurt, online service providers take care of young users – the only catch is you need to tell them that you're young!

Before uploading photographs...THINK...

Think about who can view your photographs.

- Are the photographs appropriate?
- Would you be comfortable if your parents/ teachers/siblings/school principal or your future employer saw these pictures?

If the answer to the above questions is 'no', don't upload those pictures.

Before uploading photographs ....think....

Don't broadcast your location

'Checking in' on Facebook or using the locator service on 4Square is becoming a rage in the digital world. Most people are blindly following the trend without realizing the risk involved in activating such a service.

Spare a moment and think – Would you want a stalker to know exactly where to find you? Or, how wise is it to tell a thief that you're not at home or that you would be travelling for the next two weeks?

Staying safe online is more than just having a strong password; it's actually about sharing enough without revealing too much!

Don't broad cast your location

Review your friend list

Look closely as you go through your friend list. If you realize that you've accepted friend requests from strangers (i.e. people you don't know in real life) simply put their name into a search engine and see what comes up. 'Un-friend' them at the slightest suspicion and trust your instincts.

'The Mutual friend'

You receive a friend request from someone you don't know, but seeing that you have a high number of mutual friends, you accept the request. However, you have never met or corresponded with this person earlier.

Later, as you review your friend list, you see an unfamiliar name and wonder who that is. You visit their profile and notice they do not live in the same city as you or your friends; they have interests completely unrelated to yours. They possibly have a very high number of Facebook friends and the 'mutual friends' were probably coincidental. If you ask your friends who the person is, each one would probably say they just accepted the 'friend request' under the assumption that the individual was a friend of the other. You should delete this 'mutual friend' from your list of friends.

An "Internet Friend" you need to watch out for....

During chat sessions, some "friends" will not ask you any direct questions but will keep revealing little things about themselves. For instance, they may say "I'm going for a two week vacation to Europe" or "I'm alone until my mother comes home @ 4:30". You might unknowingly respond by revealing valuable personal information and eventually get the shock of your life when this 'Internet Friend' shows up at your doorstep!

Be very cautious. This person has pieced together nuggets of information that you revealed inadvertently and now he/she has access to your personal data.

Don't assume that a stranger who has been chatting with you for a long time is now your "close friend"; **he/she is a stranger who knows so much about you because you revealed that information.**

Use a safe screen name

While using instant messaging or chat rooms, it's wise to use a screen name instead of your real name.

Use a safe screen name. A screen name such as vinay2002 reveals the user's personal identity (gender and presumably, the year of birth) to strangers. It is safer to use screen names that don't give away any personal information.

How to choose a safe screen name:

- Your screen name should be gender neutral.
- It should not include any part of your real name.
- Select random numbers which do not reveal your age/date of birth/address/telephone number.
- Don't use the name of your city or locality or school.
- You could use the name of your favorite book or movie.

Use a safe screen name.

4

SMART STEPS TO DEAL WITH ONLINE PREDATORS

The Internet gives people the freedom to be whoever they want to be and create an 'online identity' which could be very different from what they actually are. In the real world it might be impossible for a 40 year old man to pretend to be a 14 year old girl. But when it comes to cyber space, this kind of impersonation is possible.

In the cyber world, there is a small percentage of people, who pretend to be someone they aren't. They have the freedom to be whoever they want to be. Many dangerous people misuse this freedom to befriend youngsters and are called online predators.

Their ultimate objective is to build trust and gain enough information about their targets, until they can either arrange a meeting or track them down.

Please be very cautious! Don't assume that the strangers you first meet online are really who they claim to be, because it is practically impossible to make out who you are chatting with. I reiterate - don't accept friend requests (on social networking sites) from people you have never met in the real world.

Beware of online predators

How to recognize a "Bad Person" online

Simple signs to watch out for and recognize a "bad person" online:

- They want you to keep their 'friendship' with you a closely guarded secret.
- They keep reminding you not to tell your parents or family about your conversations/ activities with them.

- They make you uncomfortable.
- They ask you too many questions.
- They insist that you send them a picture of yourself.
- They often express their 'desire' to meet you.
- They say they really understand what you're going through.
- They say they share the same interests/hobbies.
- They won't disclose how they know so much about you.
- They try to win your trust by saying that they feel the same way about things as you do.

Hot to recognize a bad person online

Use a webcam wisely

Online predators often encourage their unsuspecting victims to use webcams. If anyone asks you to do anything on a web cam that makes you feel uncomfortable, it is very important to STOP, switch off and report the matter to a trusted adult immediately.

Use a webcam wisely

Say 'NO' to Real Life Meetings

The most important Internet Safety Rule is that you should never arrange a face-to-face meeting with anyone you know only via the Internet. If you are very keen to meet someone and you are sure that the person is trustworthy, inform your parents or a trusted adult. Then, talk to this person over the phone or ask your parent to arrange for a daytime meeting in a public place and make sure that your parent or a trusted adult accompanies you.

Say "no" to real life meetings

Beware of Internet Trolls

There are people in the virtual world who deliberately try to make you angry online. Such people are referred to as 'Internet Trolls' and they try to cause trouble in cyber space by being rude or argumentative. It is best to ignore Internet Trolls because the more you respond to their messages, the more they will offend you.

Beware of Internet trolls

Avoid going online when you're sad or angry/upset with a sibling/parent/friend. Decisions we make are often linked to our emotional state. In an overwhelmed state one tends to ignore Internet Safety Rules and can land up in a dangerous situation. Invariably, emotions stop us from thinking clearly about the consequences of our actions. So stay away from cyberspace when you're experiencing negative emotions; you could consider going out to play or visiting a friend or reading a book, instead.

Avoid going online when sad

5

SMART STEPS TO AVOID "SEXTING"

"Sexting" (or exchanging sexually explicit images via text messages or electronic devices) has become a popular activity among teenagers.

The biggest problem with "sexting" is that the moment you 'send' the text or image you've lost control over that text/image; you have 'sent' that control to whoever receives your text/image. In the heat of the moment, you think that's not a problem because you trust the receiver. Maybe now, yes! But what about when you are no longer a couple/friends and he/she decides to share your photo/message?

In fact, a new form of harassment termed as 'Revenge Porn' is being used to publicize the uglier side of a relationship when a friendship turns bitter. Pictures of the victims' private moments are linked to their social media profile for the world to view. Before long, everyone they know (and everyone that they don't know) would have seen the images that were meant for one person's eyes only. By then, the consequences of 'sexting' have spilled out of cyberspace to mess up their real lives and there's nothing they can do about it.

Take a minute before you send an intimate message or photo to anyone and ask yourself if you would post it on your own Facebook wall. If the answer is 'No', then don't send it to anyone. It might come back to haunt you later. Friends can become enemies, so don't leave them with any powerful weapons to use against you later.

Further, one must know that forwarding of very personal and private nude/semi-nude pictures is an OFFENCE under the IT Act Section 354. So, what appears like a prank or fun is actually a CRIME!

Avoid "sexting"

How to deal with unwanted 'sexts'

- The first thing to do is to simply ignore and delete unwanted sexts.
- If the messages are from someone you don't know, you could respond with, 'You have the wrong number'.
- If the messages are from someone you know, clearly communicate that you are not interested. Be firm!
- If the messages persist, block that contact.
- In case you feel the need to file a police complaint, talk to a trusted adult and remember to save the 'sexts' as evidence.

Loopholes in Snapchat

Snapchat, a photo messaging application that allows users to take photos / record videos and send them to a controlled list of recipients, is rather unique. The "Snaps" once viewed will be deleted from the recipient's device and from Snapchat's servers, within a time limit (1 to 10 seconds) set by the sender. This unique feature gives users a false sense of security when they send nude/semi nude pictures, since they think that their pictures will self destruct within seconds. Users are tempted to share any kind of photographs because they believe that it can't be forwarded, saved or tagged on a social networking site.

- Unfortunately, they are too naïve to see the loopholes.
- A screen shot of the image can be taken before it gets hidden.
- A picture of the image can be clicked using another phone before it self-destructs.
- It is also possible to download simple software that allows iPhone users to save videos on to their hard drives.
- There are certain ways of recovering deleted files.
- Snapchat's own privacy agreement states that "we cannot guarantee that deletion of any message always occurs within a particular timeframe. We also cannot prevent others from making copies of your messages (e.g., by taking a screenshot)."

6

SMART STEPS FOR MANAGING YOUR ONLINE REPUTATION

Online reputation has two facets- what you post about yourself and what others post about you.

You need to remember – what goes online, stays online...forever! Whatever you post on the Internet can be viewed by a vast invisible audience and unlike humans, the Internet doesn't forget. Things that you do in cyber space when you're younger stick to you and will affect you when you grow older.

Poor online behavior can have a serious impact on your real life and your future. Your teachers and friends in school/college create an impression about you based on how you behave in class. Similarly, college admission officers, teachers and professors, future employers, friends and acquaintances judge you by what they see online.

Online reputation management is now considered an important life skill that you need to learn in this digital age. The importance of a clean online image cannot be overlooked. Manage it well by keeping your posts, messages and comments clean. If someone 'tags' you in an unflattering social media post, you should remove the tag as soon as possible.

Don't share too much about your real life in the virtual world

Sharing too much about your personal life – relationships, areas of interest, future plans, outings, vacations, new experiences etc. - on social networking sites may not be a very good idea. You might be tempted to tell the whole world about things happening in your life, but eventually you'll realize that it leads to loss of privacy and makes you vulnerable. Online friends (who know you offline, as well as those who don't) might take advantage of all the information that you've shared. **Once it's online, it's public and the worst part is - it's your own doing!**

Track your digital footprint

Your digital footprint is a record of your online activities. Each time you enter the digital world, you leave behind a trail or a footprint of all your interactions including status updates, posting comments, visiting websites, sending emails, attachments, uploading videos/images, playing online games, chatting etc.

Try typing your own name or email address into a search engine like Google. It will list out all your online interactions.

If you have posted anything in a forum (online group discussions) using your name or email address, it could enable someone to find more information about you – such as your areas of interest, your profile, family, friends and much more.

It is not just what you post about yourself that matters, what others post about you also contributes to your digital footprint and all of this creates your online reputation.

Remember that most Universities/Recruiters check the digital footprint of the applicant before granting admission/job. Your online image gets automatically linked to your offline image, so the importance of a clean digital footprint cannot be underestimated.

7

SMART STEPS TO DEAL WITH CYBERBULLYING

– Be neither 'Victim' nor 'Bully'!

Be careful about your online comments and posts. Sometimes you may not intend to hurt someone but your jokes or pranks can end up offending someone, rather than amusing them. This is especially true when comments are posted on a social networking platform.

Take a minute before you comment or send a message to a friend and think about the repercussions it may have. Put yourself in his/her shoes....your words could traumatize your friend 24x7. I'm sure you'd never want to do that!

Weapons of a CYBER BULLY

- Nasty messages/abusive language
- Threatening messages
- Embarrassing comments
- Hurtful remarks
- Unwanted videos/images

Say 'no' to cyber bullying

A cyber bully often says things online that he/she would not even think of saying face to face. Hidden behind the computer screen, cyber bullies misuse the liberty and think that they can get away with anything - humiliating the victim, spreading rumors about the victim, posting morphed photographs of their target, sending pornographic videos/images etc.

What they probably fail to see is the trauma of the victim - a trauma that haunts the victim even when he/she is not online and sometimes drives him/her to take steps as drastic as suicide.

Learn to deal with Cyber Bullies

If you are being bullied online follow a simple 3 step policy- **IBR**.

I for Ignore- Simply ignore messages that make you uncomfortable and stop online conversations that make you uneasy. The more you respond to such messages, the more you'll be attacked.

B for Block- If you're unable to ignore, you must immediately 'block the bully' and ensure that they cannot contact you again. Most social networking sites allow you to block a selected contact. You could also contact your Internet Service Provider (ISP) or phone company and ask them to block the person who is bullying you.

R for Report- If the problem persists, 'report abuse' on the website, wherever possible or you could report the matter to a trusted adult or parent or a teacher.

If you are being bullied....It's not your fault!

Unfortunately, most cases of cyber bullying go unreported because the victims are too afraid to mention anything about it to anyone. They're scared that their parents might blame them and would restrict their online activities. In some case, the victim is threatened by the aggressor and feels too embarrassed to talk about it.

Remember - if you are being bullied online, it is not your fault! Please tell your parents or teachers about it, just the way you would if you were being bullied in school.

Keep evidence

If you receive hurtful texts or emails or 'chat' messages, you must copy and save them on your computer, as a 'screen shot'. These saved messages serve as strong evidence when you report the bullying as a cyber crime. In the light of the evidence that you provide, the authorities and the police can take strict action against the bully, under Section 66A of the IT Amendment Act 2008.

Keep evidence

8

SMART STEPS TO PREVENT INTERNET ADDICTION

The inability to remove oneself from the web is termed as Internet Addiction Disorder or IAD. Today's 'wireless world' is actually increasingly wired and we're connected to the Internet all the time through a vast network of electronic media.

Symptoms of IAD:

- Choosing to be online instead of spending time with family and friends.
- Deliberately hiding online activities from parents.
- People around you complain that you spend too much time online
- You look for the slightest opportunity to log in, maybe as soon as a family member leaves you alone.
- Your thoughts are always online even when you are not!

If you are suffering from similar symptoms and feel disinterested in other activities, seek parental support and guidance or talk to a trusted adult immediately

Internet addiction

Define a time line for your online activities

How many hours do you spend online everyday? Recent research has proved that our online lives (in terms of the number of hours spent in cyberspace) are extending at an unimaginable rate and we're not even aware of it.

With the advent of smart phones we can now access the internet even on the move. This means we spend most of our time online.

It is advisable to define a time of the day and specify the number of hours you wish to spend online. You need to create a schedule for yourself and follow a discipline, just the way you balance studies and extra-curricular activities.

9

SMART STEPS FOR SAFE ONLINE FINANCIAL TRANSACTIONS

When it comes to making online financial transactions, your parents' involvement is a must. In the real world, you don't go around using their credit/debit card while shopping in a mall or spending huge amounts of cash. Follow the same policy in the virtual world – don't indulge in any kind of financial transactions such as making payments online. If you are very keen on learning about online transactions you could ask your parents to show you how and then do it under their supervision.

If you receive lottery emails watch out

There is an increasing incidence of receiving out-of-the blue e-mails proclaiming that you have won thousands or millions of dollars in a lucky draw, supposedly held in a distant country. The result of responding to such fake emails is that the 'lucky winner' ends up coughing up large sums of money as 'handling charges' or 'processing fee' or 'tax exemptions' and etc.

Warning Signs:

- **Errors**: On closer look, you will realize that the e-mail is not even addressed 'To:' you; they don't mention your name. Watch out for grammatical errors and spelling mistakes, since English is generally not their mother tongue.
- **They want details:** Sometimes names of real lotteries and banks are invoked and when you click on the URL mentioned therein, you get to access a look-alike website, similar to that of the real bank/institution/corporation. The unwary victim gets easily trapped and ends up revealing details of bank accounts and other confidential information.
- **They want your money**: Remember the prize fund doesn't exist; neither does the firm acting as the "agent' nor the bank supposedly holding the winnings. On the contrary, the only fund that does exist is the money that you would be asked to pay.

They claim that you would have to pay 'nothing for everything', but the stark reality is that the 'lucky winner' ends up paying 'everything for nothing'. There is no pot of gold at the end of the rainbow, so kindly ignore such fake lottery e-mails.

10

SMART STEPS FOR SAFER ONLINE GAMING

There is absolutely no difference between chatting online and chatting on a gaming site.

"Friends" you make while playing online games are actually strangers, since you don't know them offline. People you are playing with online, no matter how long you've been playing with them or however 'friendly' they seem to be, may not really be who they say they are.

Never meet anyone outside the game – Massive Multiplayer Online Role-playing games involve a large community of anonymous players. The biggest danger lies in the unfiltered, un-moderated online discussions that take place while playing the game. Such chatting sessions usually start with exchanging tips for improving your gaming skills but can end up very differently if you are not careful.

So you need to follow the same safety policy that you would follow while interacting with strangers on any social networking platform.

Rules for safe gaming

- Keep personal information a secret - Don't share your real name, email/home address, age, gender, pictures with other players. Playing with them does not mean they are your friends; in fact they are strangers.
- Use a vague username – one that doesn't reveal your gender, age and country of residence.
- Use an avatar instead of a real picture of yourself.
- Protect your game accounts with strong passwords. A strong password is a mix of letters, numbers & symbols and has at least eight characters....the longer, the better.
- Never share your password with anyone, not even your best friend.
- Avoid downloading 'cheat codes' which claim to help you win online games since they expose your system to viruses and spyware.
- If another player is making you uncomfortable or using bad language or sending disturbing material/messages don't hesitate to block such

a player, or leave the game room immediately or mute his/her chat window.

- Downloading pirated copies of games can lead to account suspension, blocking of consoles or prosecution. Play only authorized versions of games which you've purchased from correct sources after gaining parental consent.
- While disposing (i.e. selling or donating) your gaming device, ensure that all personal information has been deleted. Delete all your account details and create a back-up by transferring data to your new device.

Rules for safer gaming

11

SMART STEPS TOWARDS BEING A GOOD NETIZEN

Your parents and teachers don't make rules because they want to limit the amount of fun you have; they make rules because they want you to be safe.

Traffic rules ensure the safety of all road users. Similarly, Internet safety rules ensure your online safety. Breaking rules can lead to accidents, abuse and sometimes even death. Following the rule book is in your own interest!

Always maintain good 'netiquette'

- Don't be rude or mean online.
- Don't use offensive or abusive language.
- Don't send/forward images and information that might embarrass or hurt someone.
- Don't use anyone's personal information to damage his/her reputation.

Be a responsible 'Netizen'!

Be a responsible netizen

12

SMART STEPS TOWARDS A SAFER CYBERSPACE

Cyberspace is a vast and varied landscape that can change with the blink of an eye. Navigating such a landscape can be difficult. Every time new ways are introduced to prevent criminals from assuming fake online identities/hacking/bullying/invading privacy/ sexting, they find new ways to get around these protective measures.

By now you would have realized that there are a lot of things in cyberspace that are potentially risky. The information provided here is not meant to deter you from availing the benefits of the Internet. However, no apologies are offered if this information has scared you or made you think twice before uploading something. In fact if it has managed to do so, the purpose of this book has been fulfilled!

Now that you're aware of the smart steps that you need to take in cyberspace, it's time to talk to your friends, siblings, parents and grandparents, to ensure that they too are safe online. Go ahead and spread the word...

Wishing you all a smarter and safer journey as you navigate cyberspace!

ABOUT THE AUTHOR

Pooja Malhotra is a cyber-education consultant and Internet safety expert. She spends much of her time conducting interactive sessions and workshops on Internet safety for tweens and teens. She has an incredible knack of encouraging children to be safe in cyberspace without sounding like a nagging adult, lecturing them on the do's & don'ts and dangers of the digital world.

A writer by compulsion, she has been contributing articles on 'Internet Safety' to newspapers and various online publications. After years of reiterating guidelines on how to be safe online, she decided to consolidate everything into a small, easy to follow guidebook and reach out to as many children as possible.